TIME SPACE AND DRUMS PART FOUR

JAZZ
DRUMMING
Development

TIME SPACE AND DRUMS PART FOUR

JAZZ DRUMMING Development

CONSTELLATIONS Volume 2

The Time Space & Drums Series
A Complete Program of Lessons in Professional, Contemporary Rock and Jazz Drumming Styles.

Written and Developed By:
Stephen Hawkins

Graphic Design By: Nathaniel Dasco.
Special Thanks To Linda Drouin and Ikhide Oshoma

ThinkeLife Publications

Time Space and Drums Copyright 2020 By Stephen Hawkins.

All Rights Reserved.

No part of this book may be reproduced in any form or by any electronic or mechanical means including information storage and retrieval means without permission in writing from the author.

The only exception is by a reviewer, who may quote short excerpts in a review.

Stephen Hawkins - Time Space and Drums
Visit my website at www.timespaceanddrums.com

First printing: August 2020.

ISBN: 978 1 913929 03 9

Dedicated to the late Paul Daniels and family, Martin Daniels, Trevor Daniels, Paul Mellor's, Keith, Peter Windle, Andrew Marple's, Colin Keys, Peters & Lee, Susan Maughan, Ronnie Dukes, Tom O'Connor, Les Dennis, Bob Monkhouse, Bobby Davro, Tommy Bruce, Robert Young, Sandie Gold as well as the hundreds of other people who have played a part in my life experience. Including Sphinx Entertainment, E & B Productions as well as the hundreds of fantastic personalities I have had the pleasure of working alongside over the past 35 years. Apologies for anyone I have missed, not forgetting the current reader who I hope will receive as much from their drumming as I have and more – Stephen Hawkins.

Table of Contents

DRUM ROLL, PLEASE! Getting Started 1

Lesson 1: Bass Drum Development Exercises 3

Lesson 2: Snare Drum Development Exercises 10

Lesson 3: Bass Drum Development Exercises Using the Shuffle Beat 16

Lesson 4: Snare Drum Development Exercises Using the Shuffle Beat 23

Lesson 5: Bass Drum Development Exercises Using the Swing Beat 30

Lesson 6: Snare Drum Development Exercises Using the Swing Beat 37

    RUDIMENTARY 44

  Flam 44

  Disciplined Practice Approach 44

    Featured Drummer Recommendations 46

  Conclusion 47

DRUM ROLL, PLEASE! Getting Started

If you have been following the Time Space and Drums Series, beginning with book 1 through to this one, then congratulations are in order! By now, you should be pretty good at playing rock style rhythms. Having said that, there is still a long way to go if you wish to succeed even further and to enhance the existing foundation.

If your completely new to this series, I highly recommend that, at the very least, you begin by completing book 2 before attempting the exercises within this book. Unless, of course, you're an intermediate drummer looking to gain a little more knowledge in the jazz style drumming arena.

Once you have mastered the contents of book 2, the next step is to develop your skills with the basic jazz rhythms from book 2. The 12/8 Triplet Beat, The Shuffle Beat, and The Swing Beat.

As before, scan through the book to get an understanding of the written exercises from a purely theoretic point of view. Then listen to the audio download files once as you follow the exercises in this book. You can download the audio demonstrations via the link at the end of this section.

Next, listen to the exercise you're studying and practice it until it becomes part of you. Perfect each exercise as you go. There is no need to rush, so make sure you are comfortable with each exercise before going forward.

For the most part, I have demonstrated the exercises within this book with the RH on the HH. It is therefore up to you to play them all again with the RH on the ride cymbal, playing beats 1, 2, 3 and 4 on the LF HH. You should also play the Swing Beat rhythms, playing the LF on beats 2 and 4 only, with your RH on the ride cymbal and again on the HH. This will produce an open HH swing beat.

Don't be tempted to miss out any of the parts I have asked you to do for yourself. It is an important and integral part of your playing and learning experience. You will be using these skills throughout your drumming career, so rewrite them in a manuscript book with your hand played on the ride cymbal.

As always, perfection is the name of the game, so have patience and enjoy yourself. Good Luck.

Stephen Hawkins

Free Audio Demonstrations

You should visit the following URL to download audio demonstrations of every exercise in this book as soon as possible. You will then receive additional tips and guidance through the included essence emails.

www.timespaceanddrums.com/tsd-4de.html

As usual, you can now skip to the rudiment section on page 43 and then, after practicing the rudiment, you can return here to begin lesson 1 starting on the next page.

Lesson 1

Bass Drum Development Exercises

The idea now is to develop the beats you learned and mastered in book 2. So, without further delay, let's begin with developing the bass drum in a 12/8 triplet time. Practice these exercises with a metronome at a slow tempo first before speeding the metronome up. Speed is not the aim; precision is.

Exercise 1

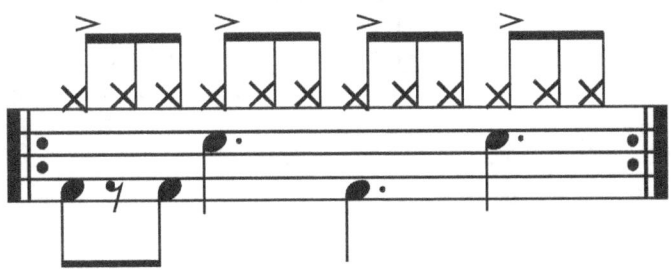

Exercise 2

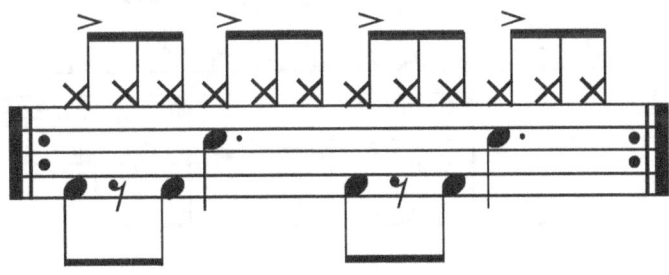

Exercise 3

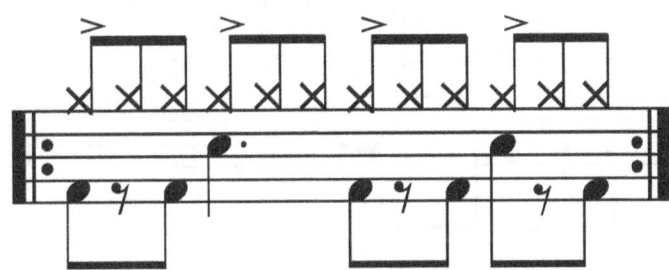

Exercise 4

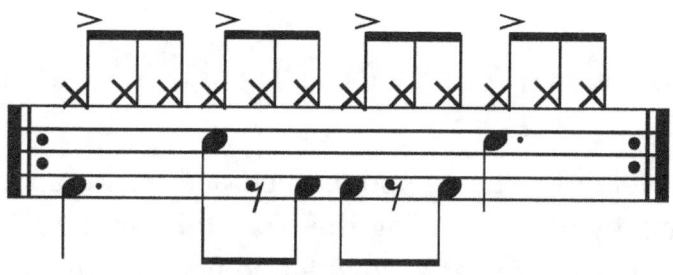

Exercise 5

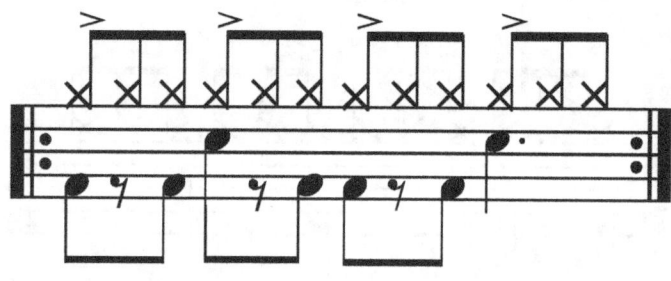

Exercise 6

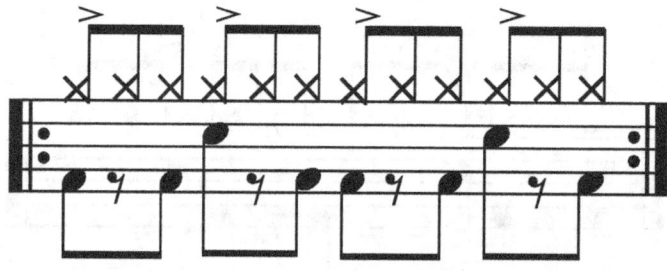

Exercise 7

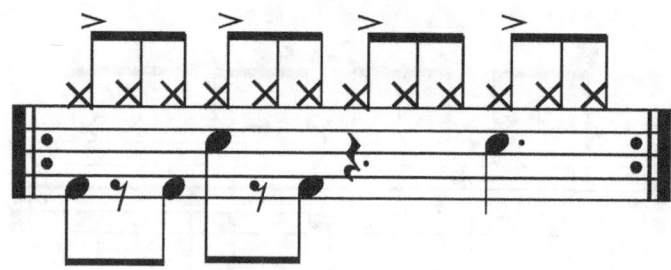

Exercise 8

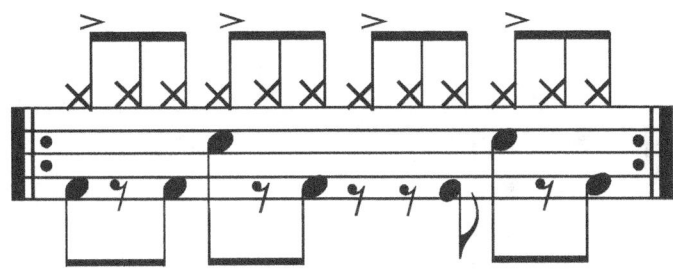

Exercise 9

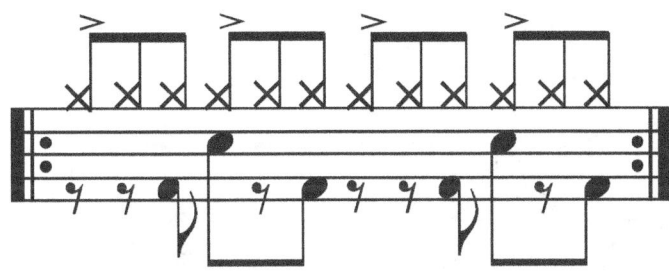

Exercise 10

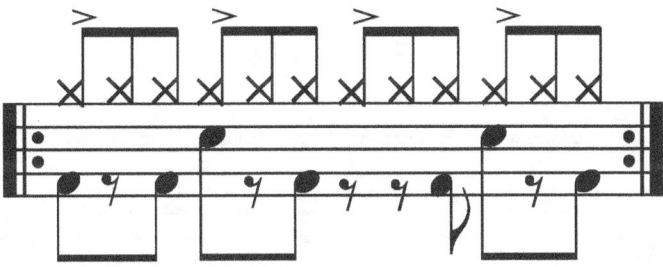

Exercise 11

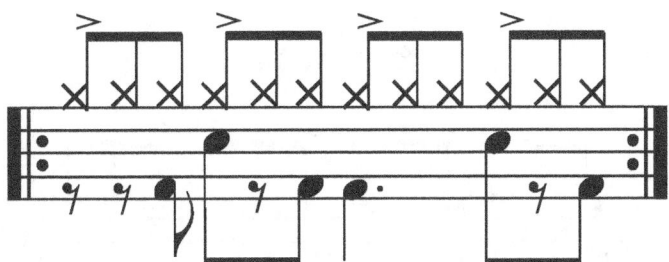

Exercise 12

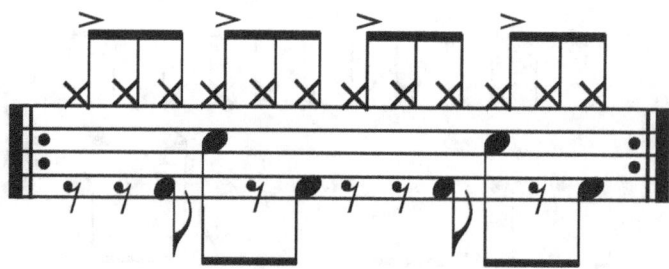

Playing the bass drum on the middle triplet.

Exercise 13

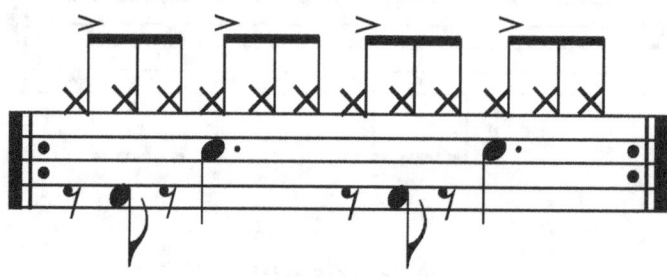

Exercise 14

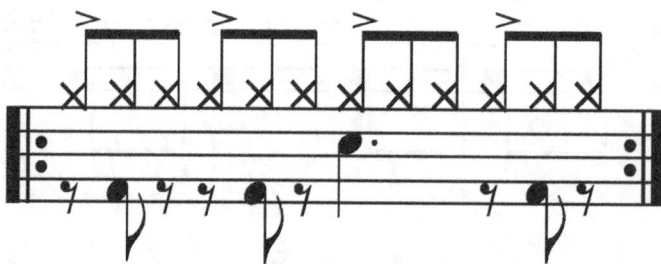

Exercise 15

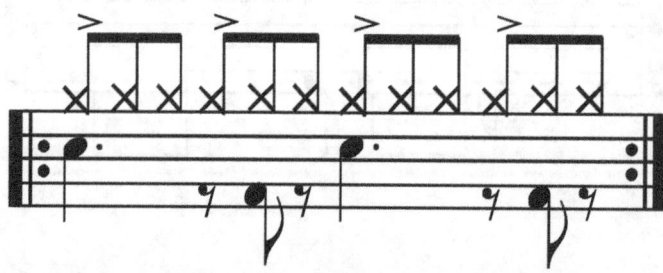

Exercise 16

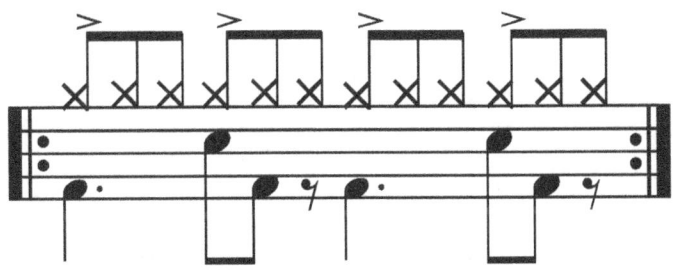

Exercise 17

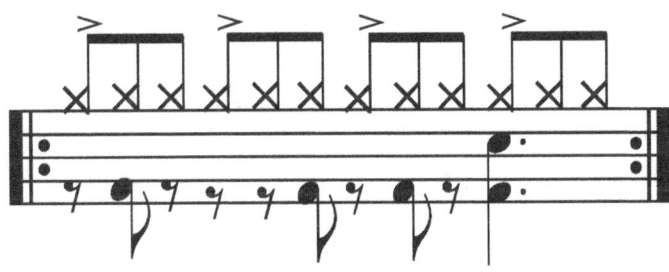

Exercise 18

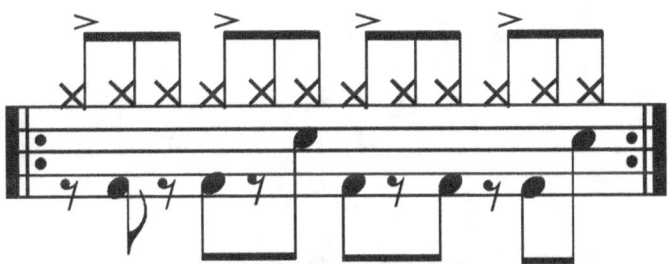

Exercise 19

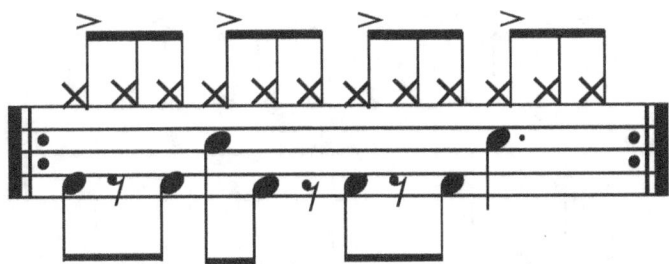

Time Space and Drums Constellations: Volume Two

Exercise 20

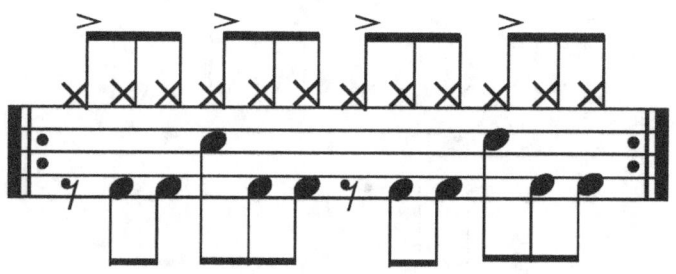

Exercise 21

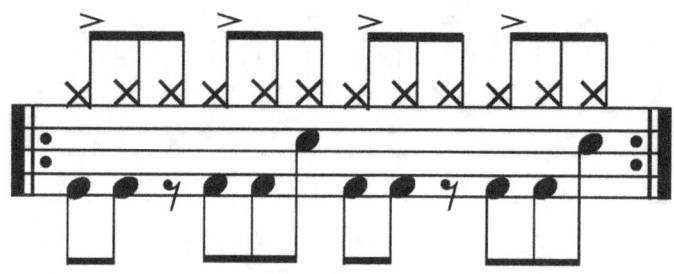

Exercise 22

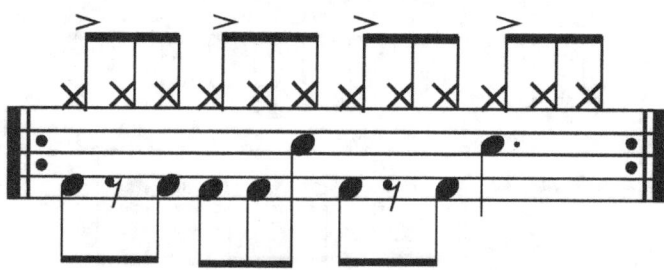

Exercise 23

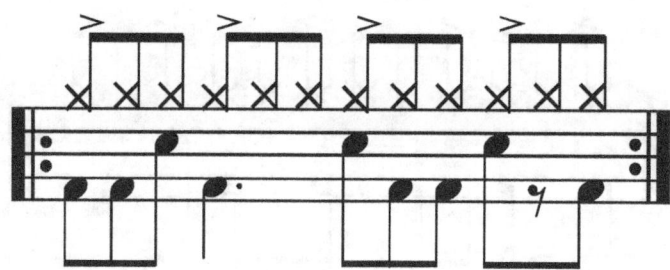

Exercise 24

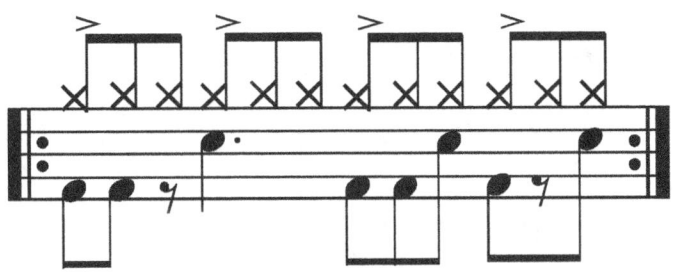

Lesson 2

Snare Drum Development Exercises

Exercise 1

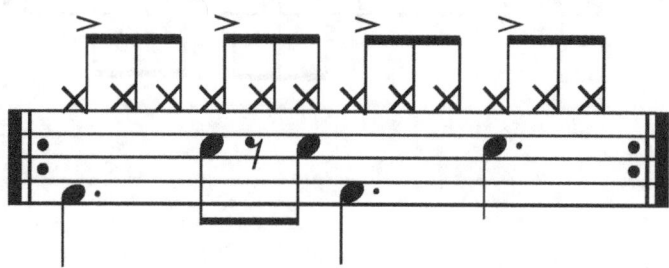

Exercise 2

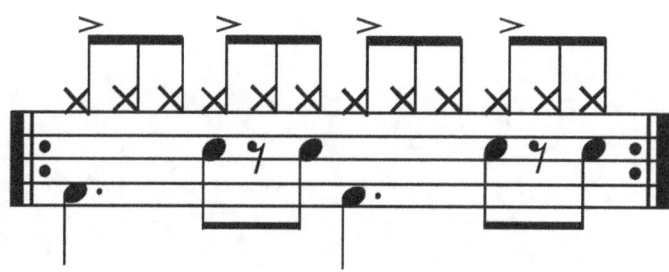

Exercise 3

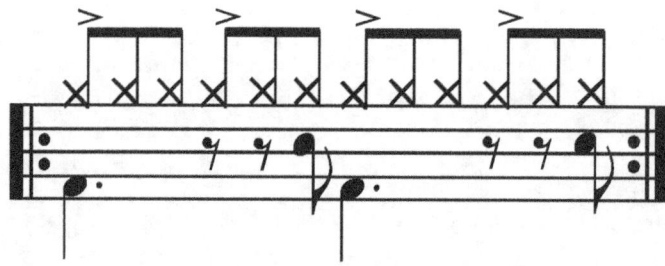

Exercise 4

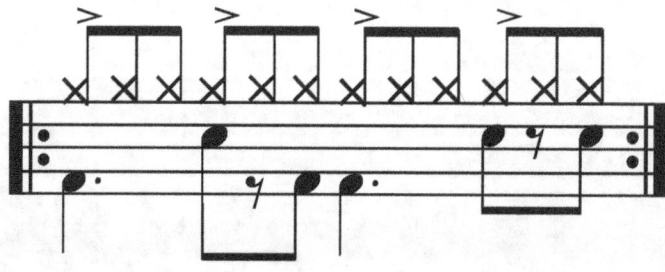

Exercise 5

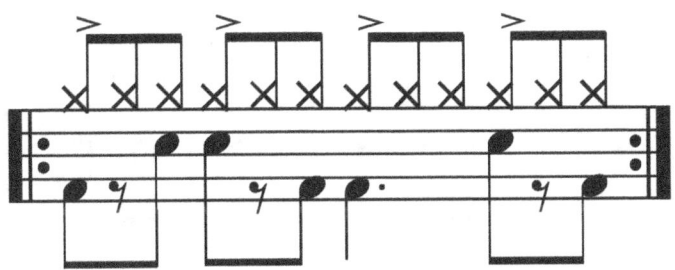

Exercise 6

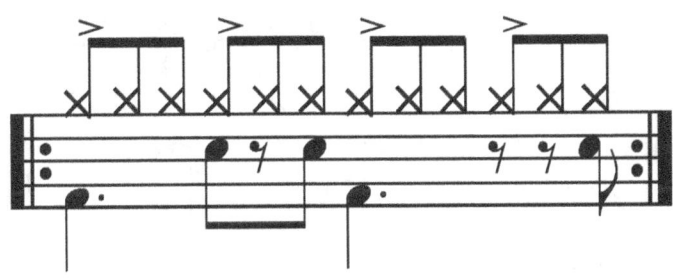

Exercise 7

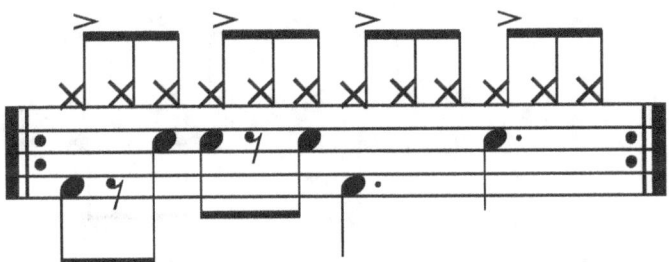

Exercise 8

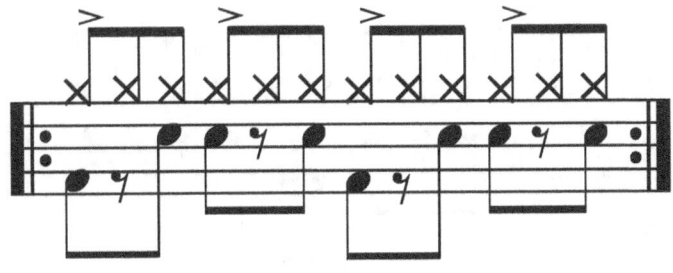

Exercise 9

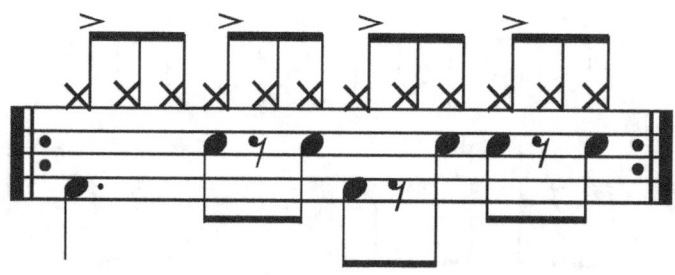

Exercise 10

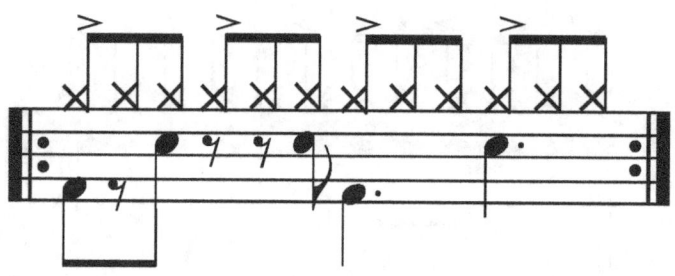

Exercise 11

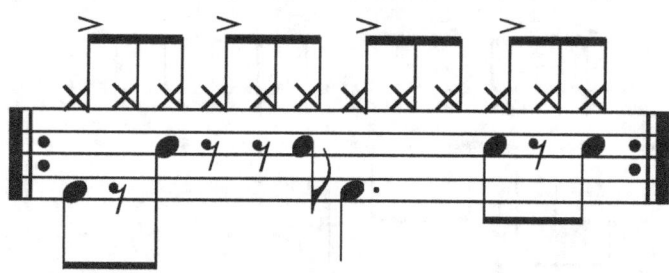

Exercise 12

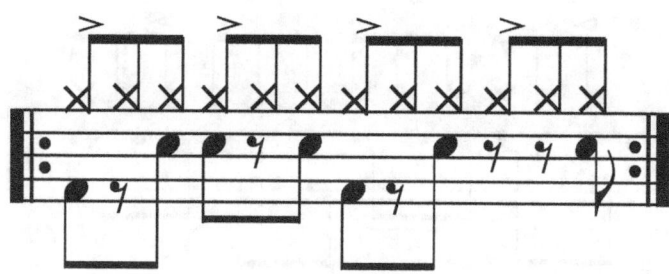

Now playing the snare drum on the middle triplet.

Exercise 13

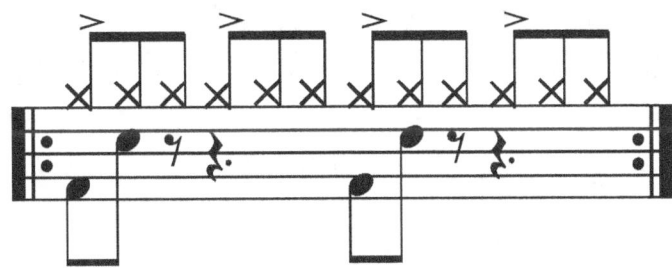

Exercise 14

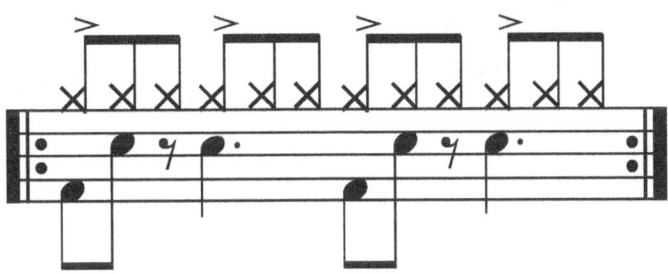

Exercise 15

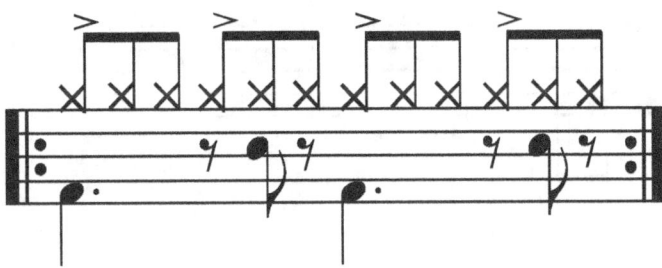

Exercise 16

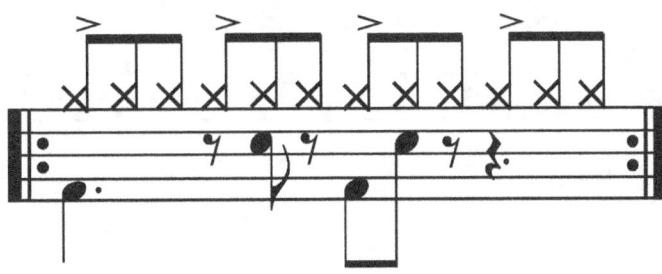

Time Space and Drums Constellations: Volume Two

Exercise 17

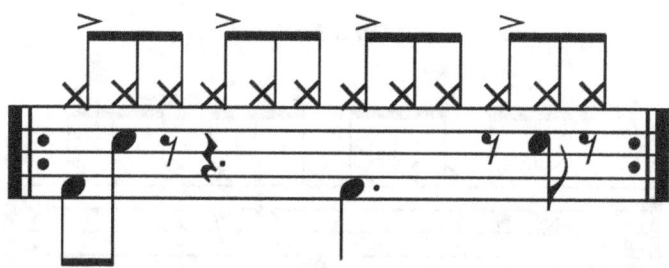

Exercise 18

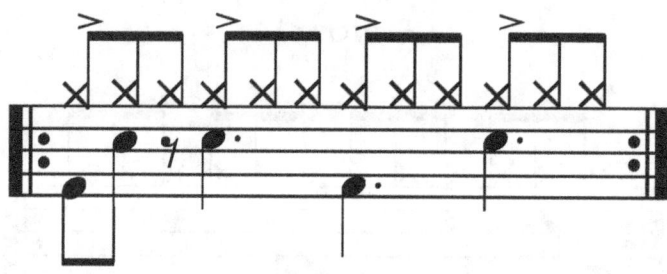

Exercise 19

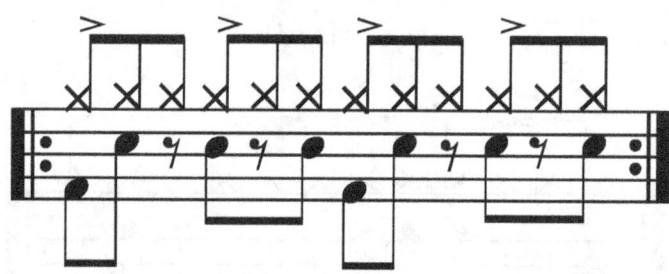

Exercise 20

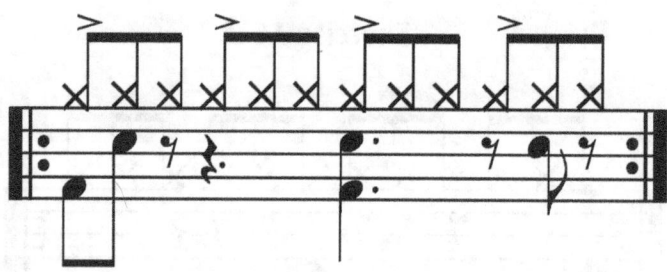

Time Space and Drums   Constellations: Volume Two

Exercise 21

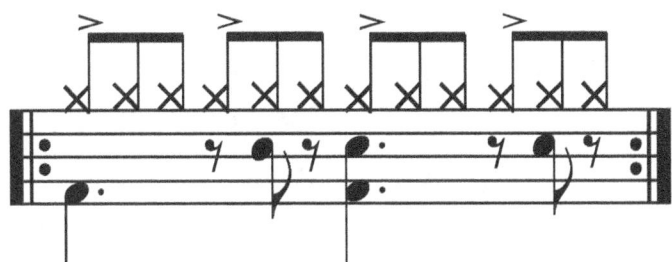

Exercise 22

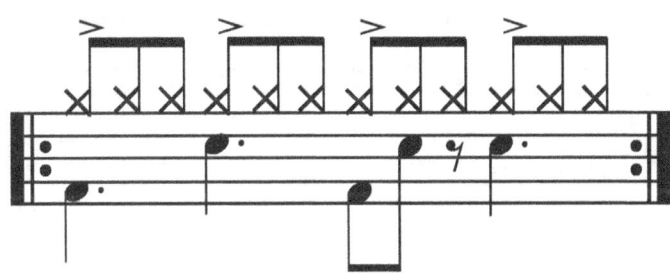

Exercise 23

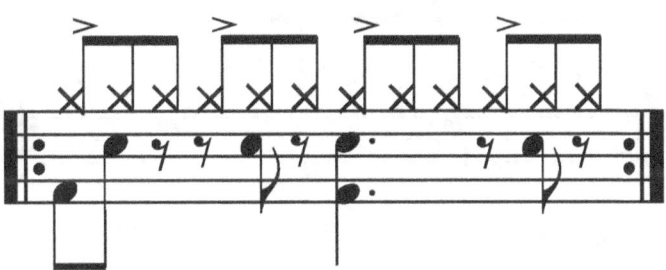

Exercise 24

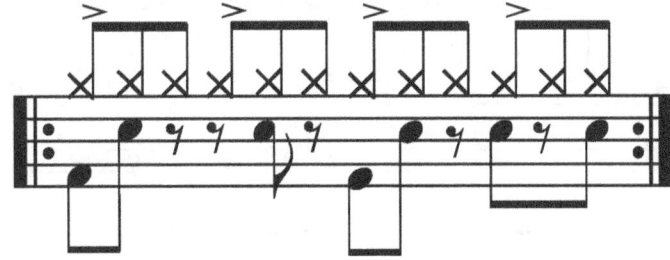

Make sure you have practiced lessons 1 and 2 well before going on to lesson 3.

Lesson 3

Bass Drum Development Exercises

Using the Shuffle Beat

The next step is to develop the bass drum using the shuffle beat.

Exercise 1

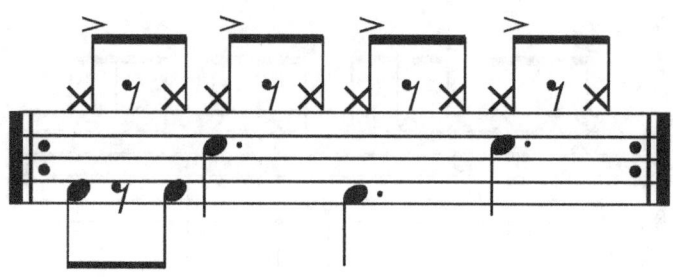

Exercise 2

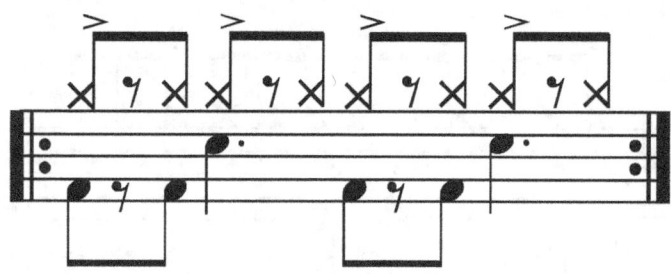

Exercise 3

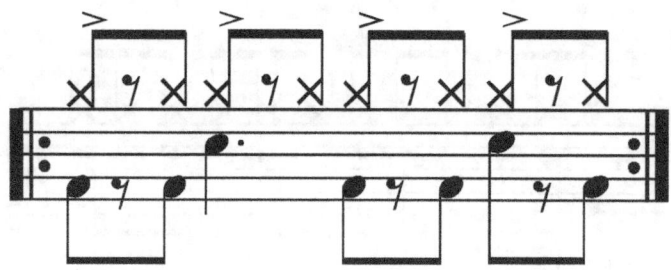

Exercise 4

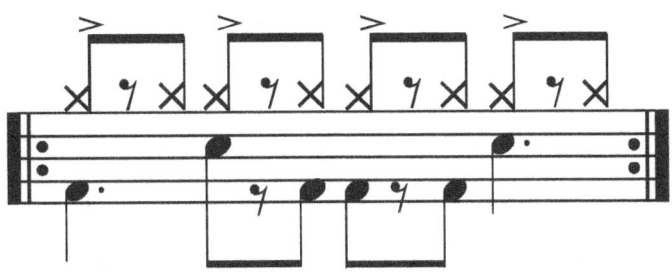

Exercise 5

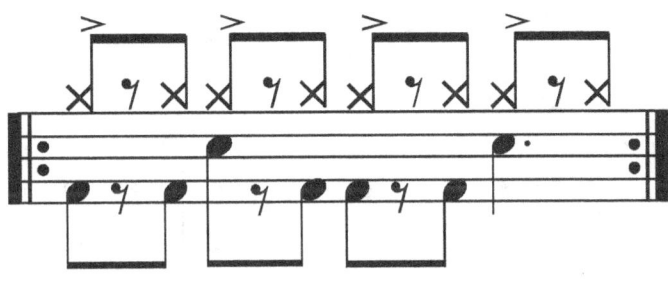

Exercise 6

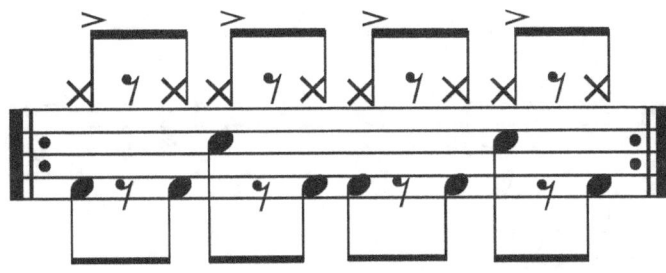

Exercise 7

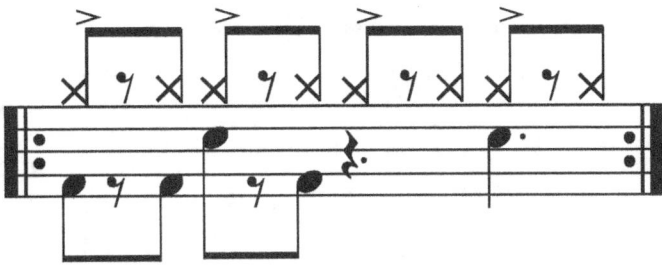

Exercise 8

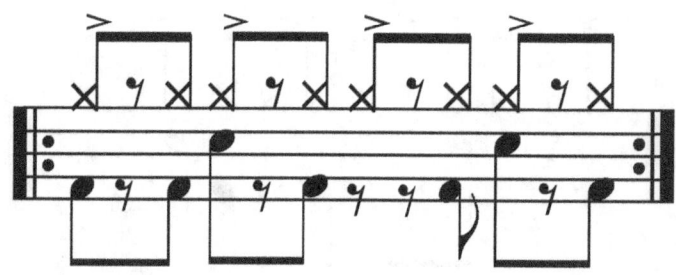

Exercise 9

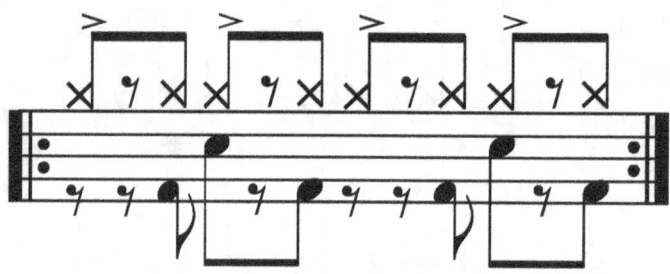

Exercise 10

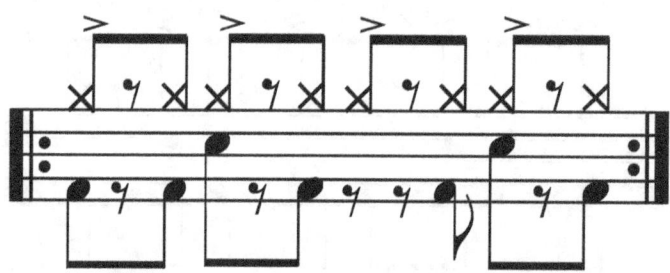

Exercise 11

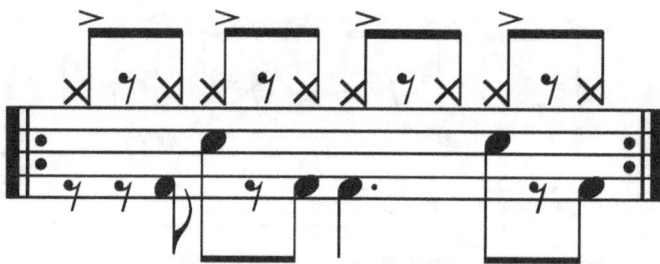

Exercise 12

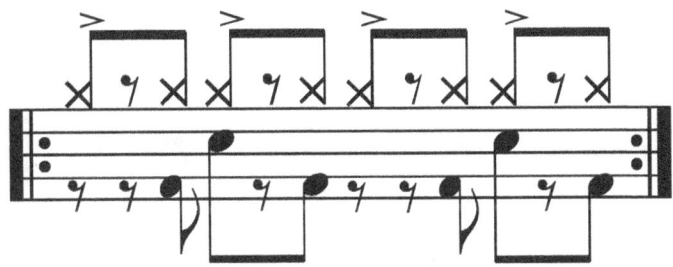

Playing the bass drum on the middle triplet.

Exercise 13

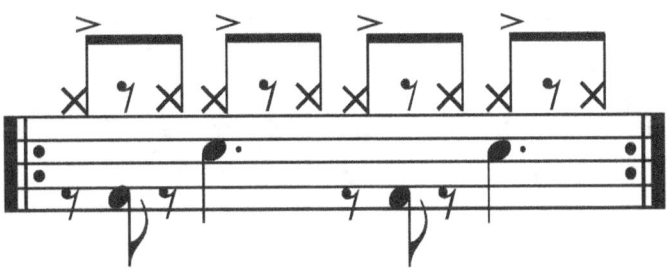

Exercise 14

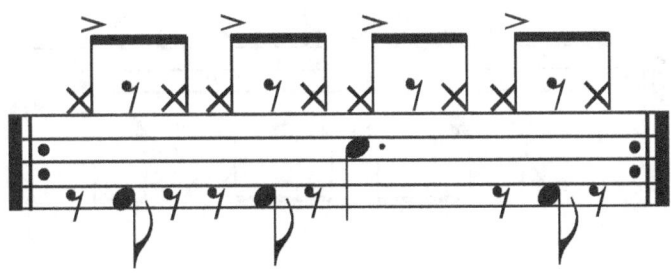

Exercise 15

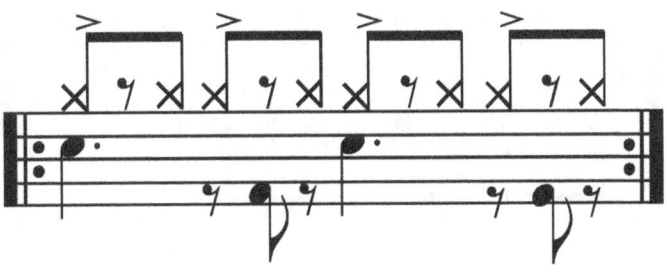

Exercise 16

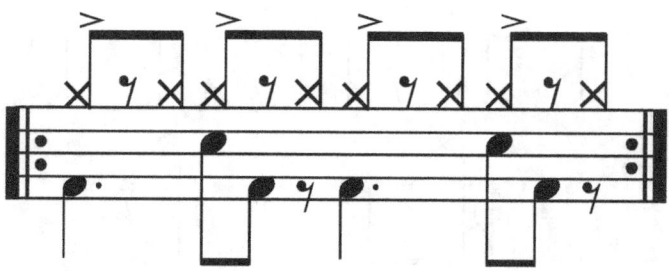

Exercise 17

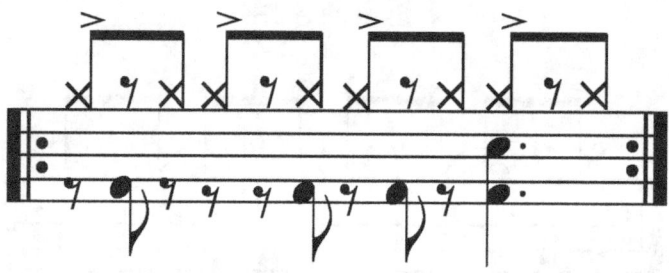

Exercise 18

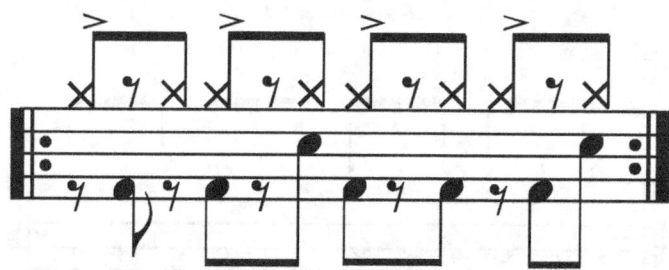

Exercise 19

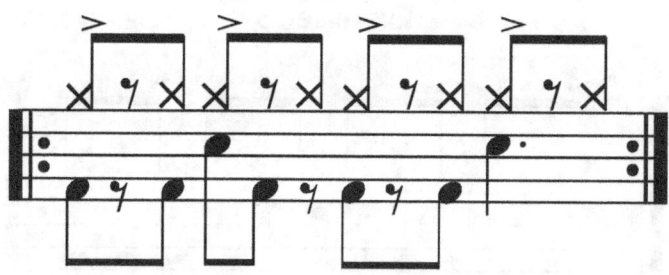

Exercise 20

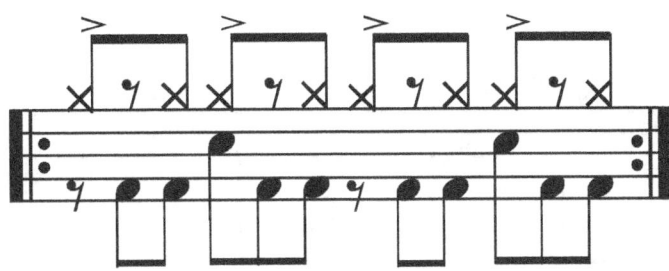

Exercise 21

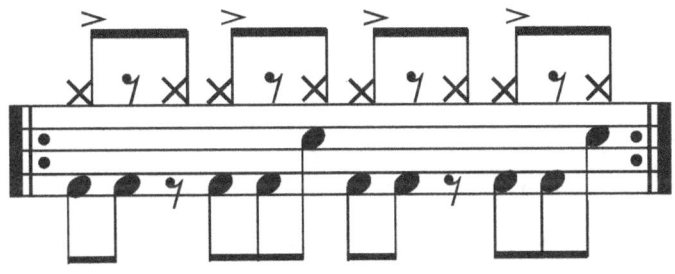

Exercise 22

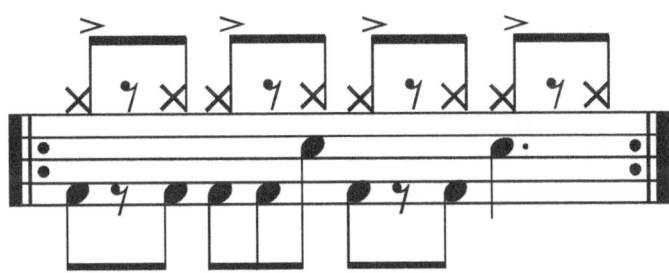

Exercise 23

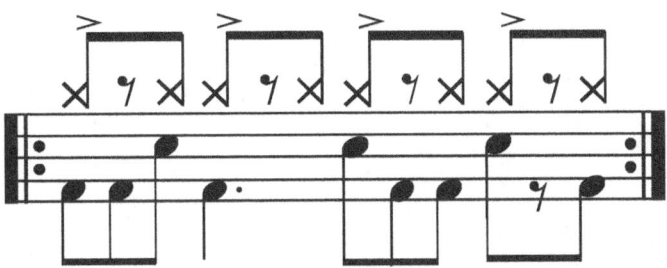

Time Space and Drums Constellations: Volume Two

Exercise 24

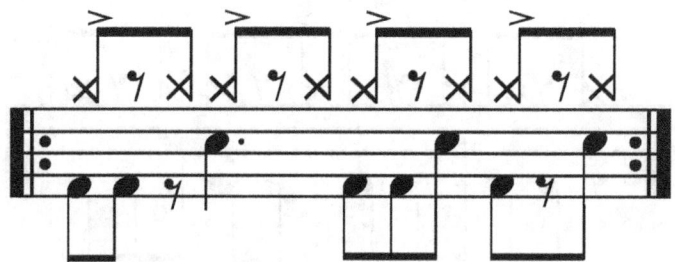

Lesson 4

Snare Drum Development Exercises

Using the Shuffle Beat

This next set of exercises involves playing the SD on the middle triplet. As with the last set of exercises, make sure that the triplets flow smoothly and evenly.

Exercise 1

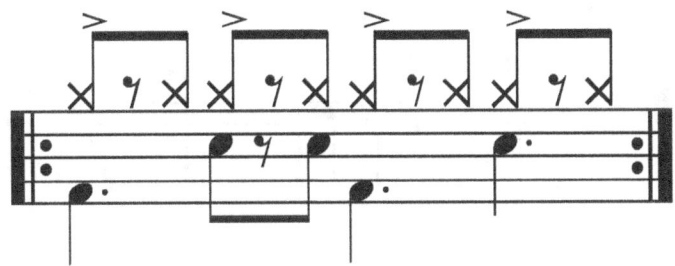

Exercise 2

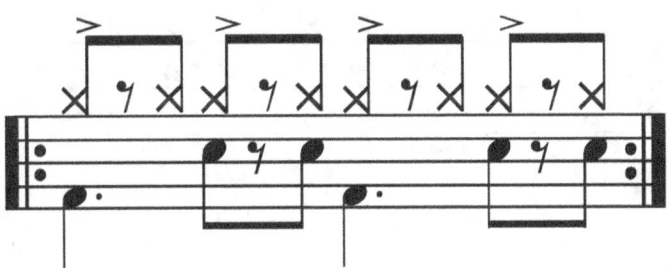

Exercise 3

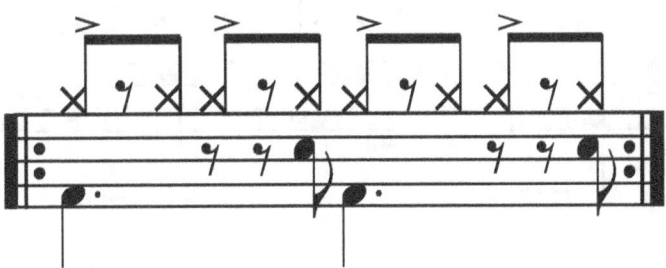

Exercise 4

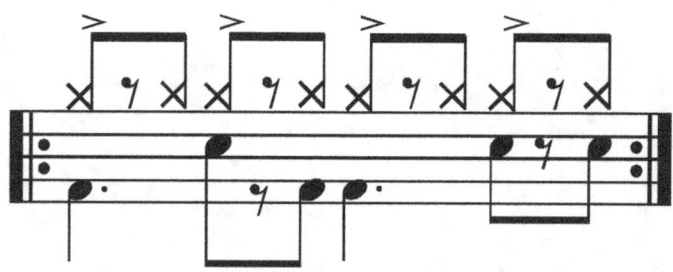

Exercise 5

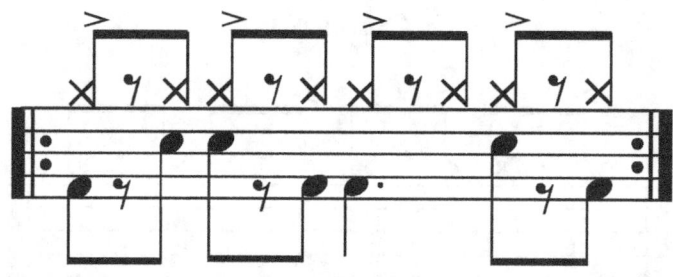

Exercise 6

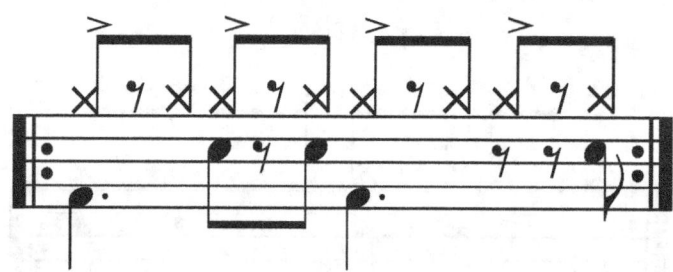

Exercise 7

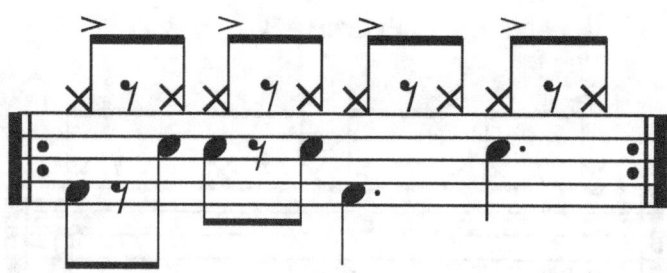

Exercise 8

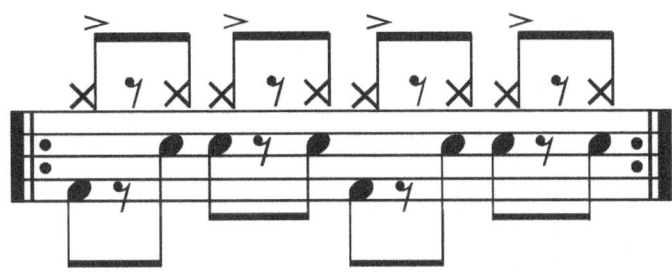

Exercise 9

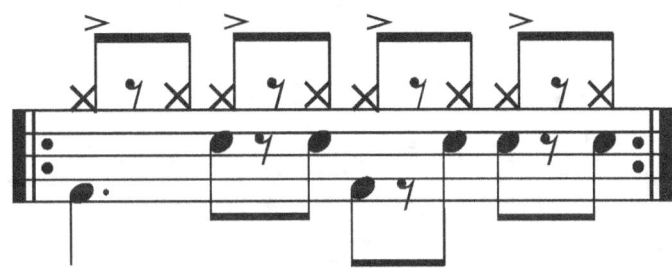

Exercise 10

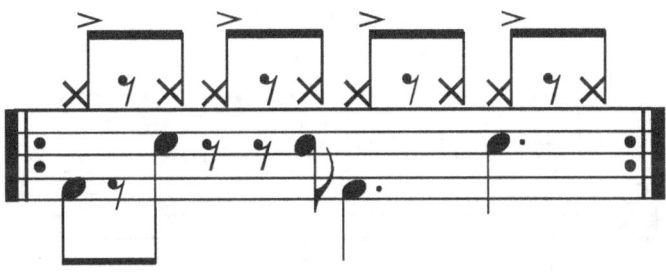

Exercise 11

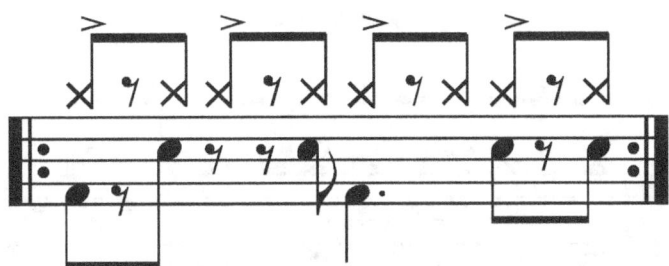

Exercise 12

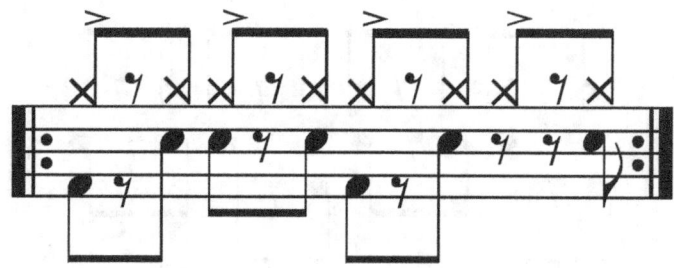

Playing the SD on the middle triplet.

Exercise 13

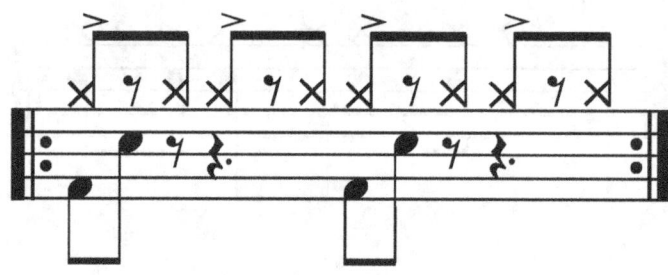

Exercise 14

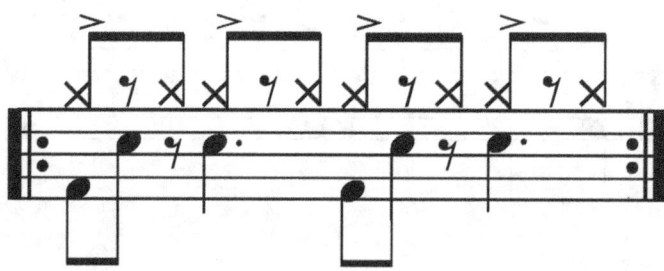

Exercise 15

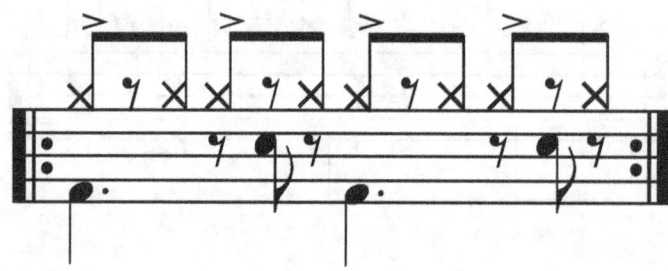

Exercise 16

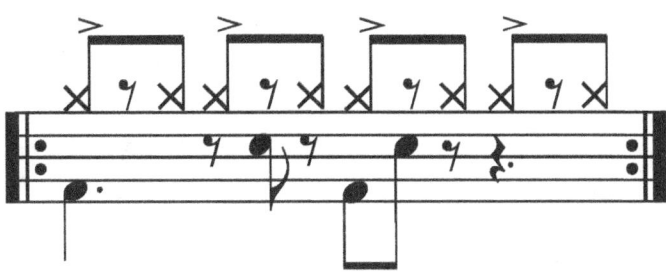

Exercise 17

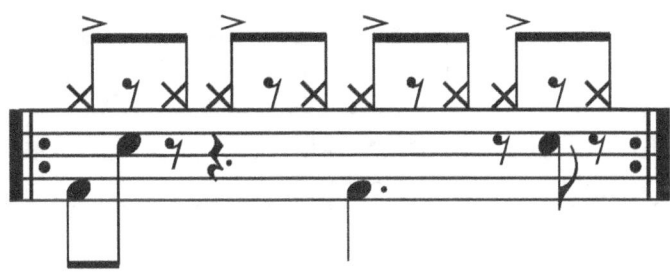

Exercise 18

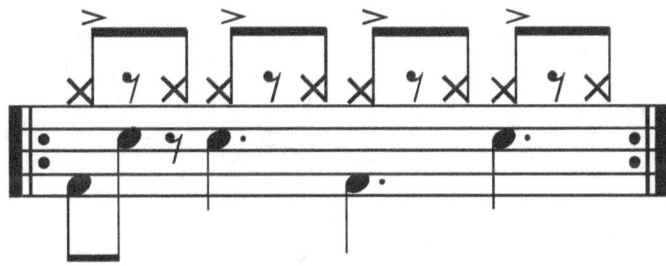

Exercise 19

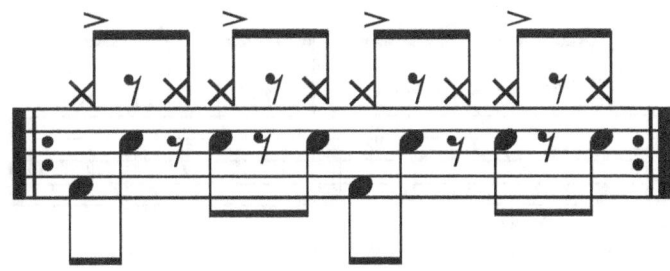

Exercise 20

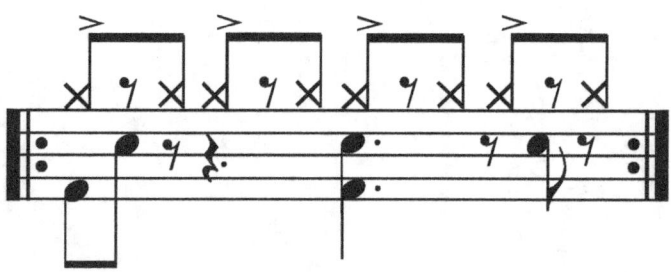

Exercise 21

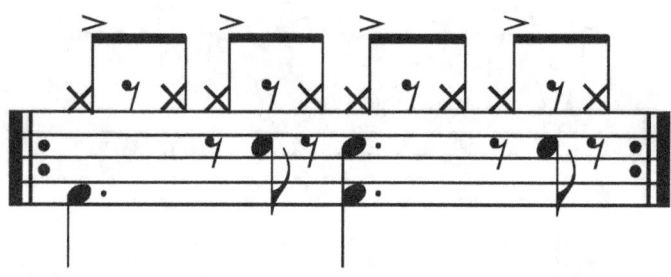

Exercise 22

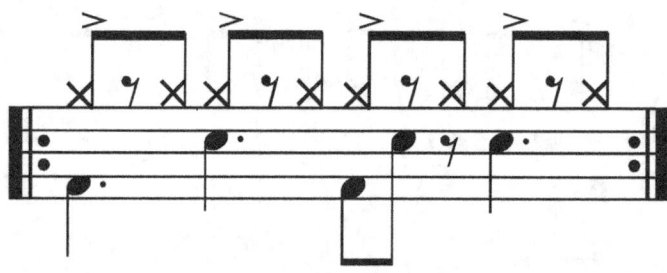

Exercise 23

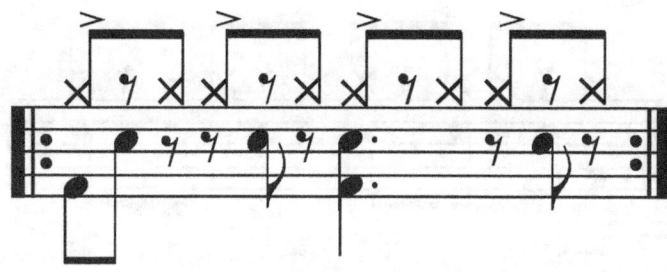

Exercise 24

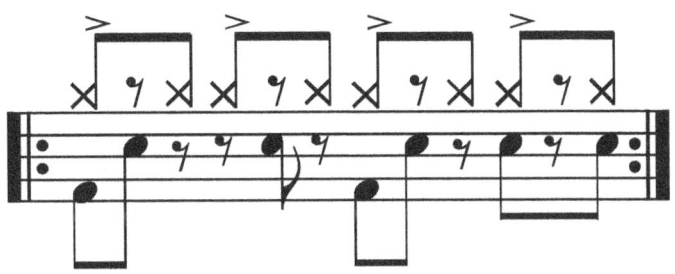

Lesson 5

Bass Drum Development Exercises

Using the Swing Beat

The next set of exercises are a little trickier; mainly because there are fewer notes played with the right-hand. This is the reason the triplet and shuffle exercises studied so far in this book are vitally important. In order to keep the flow going, you should constantly think in triplets. The slower you practice these exercises, the better and this is because it is easier to play everything at a fast tempo, and more difficult at slow tempos. In this case, you can hear the spaces (therefore the notes) easier.

Exercise 1

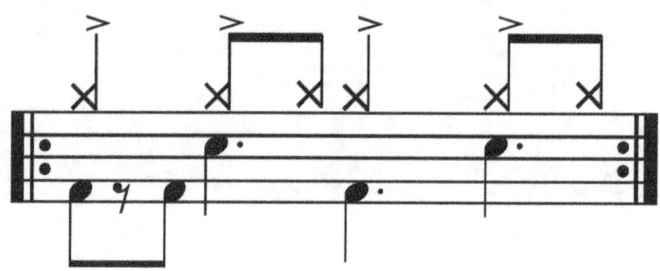

Exercise 2

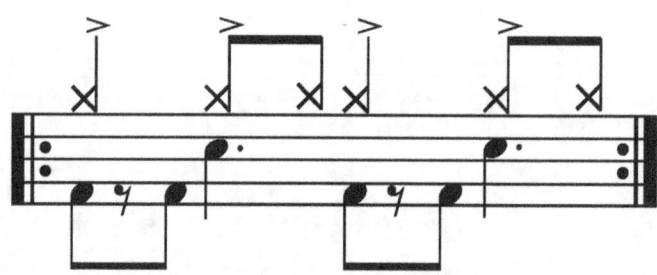

Exercise 3

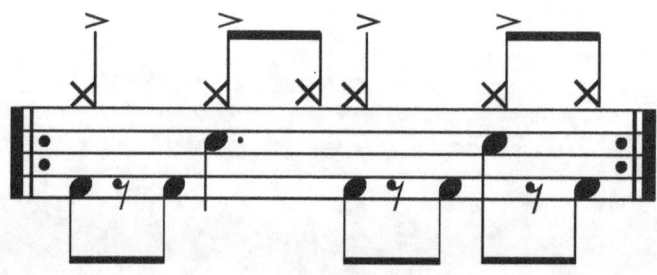

Exercise 4

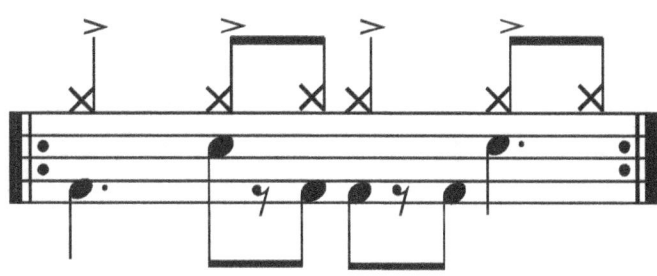

Exercise 5

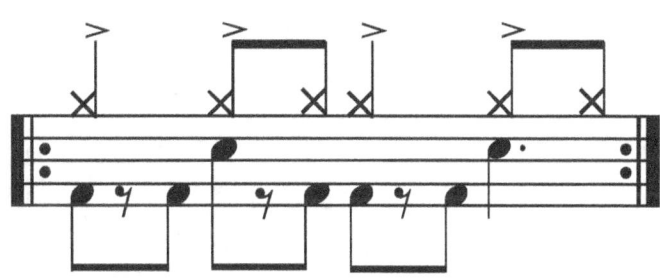

Exercise 6

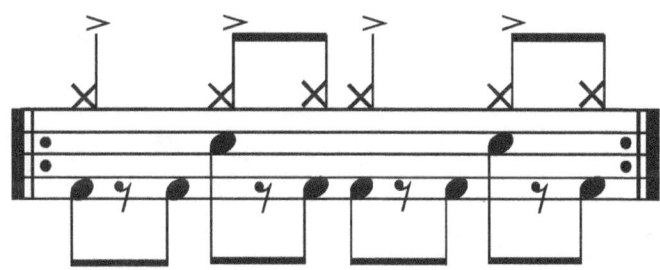

Exercise 7

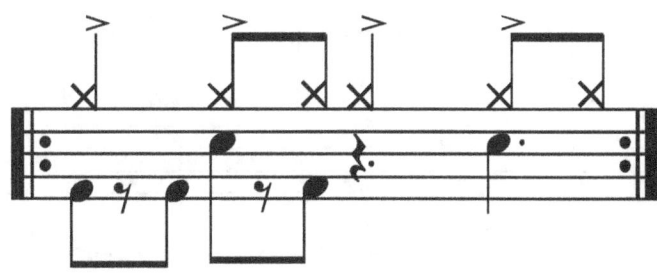

Exercise 8

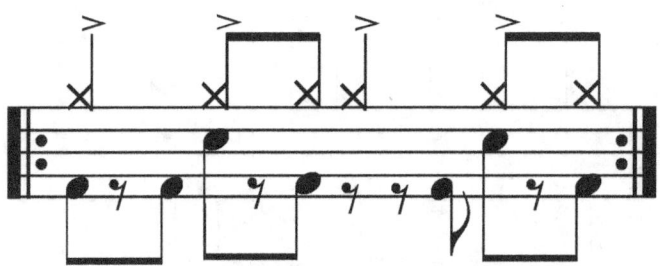

Exercise 9

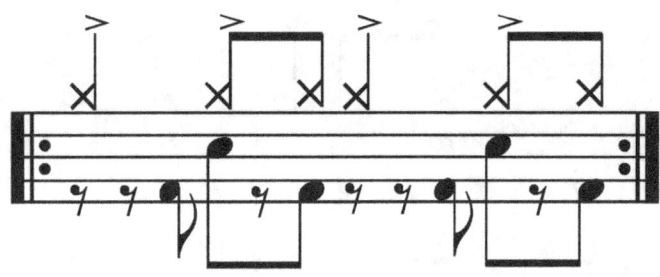

Exercise 10

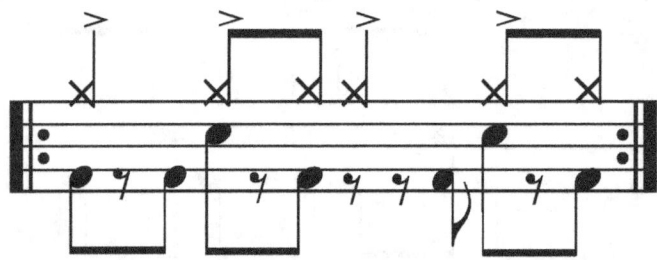

Exercise 11

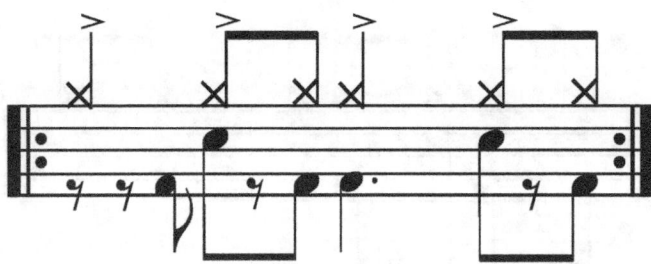

Exercise 12

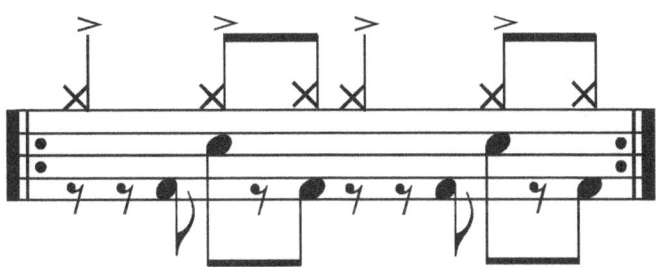

Playing the bass drum on the middle triplet.

Exercise 13

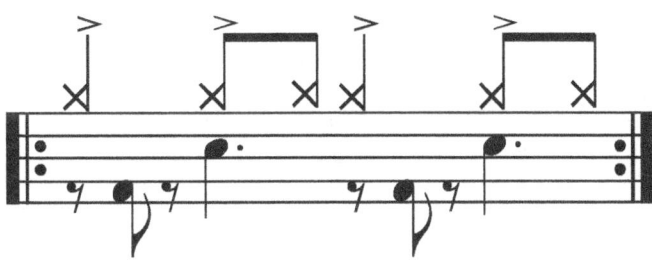

Exercise 14

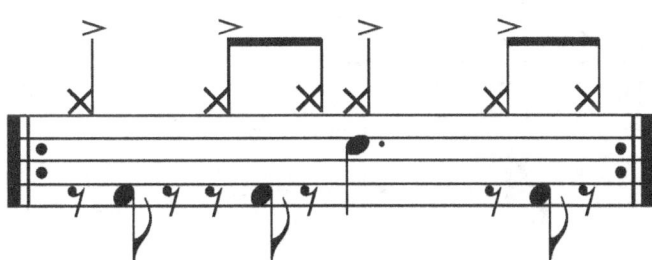

Exercise 15

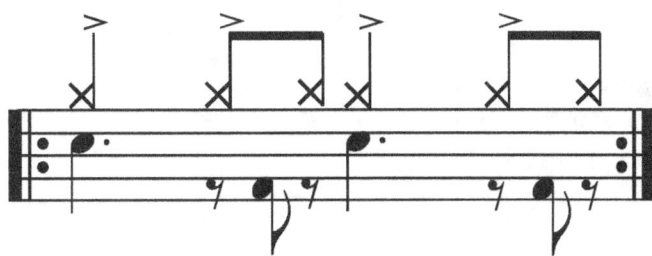

Exercise 16

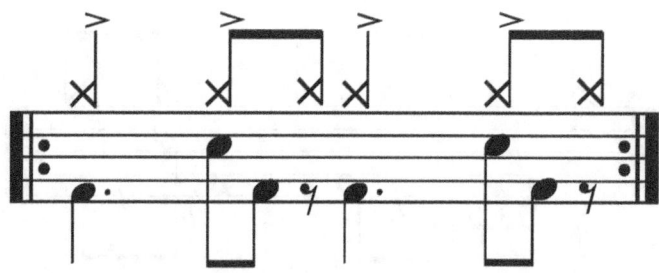

Exercise 17

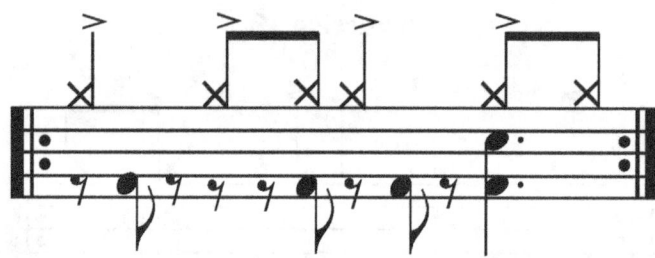

Exercise 18

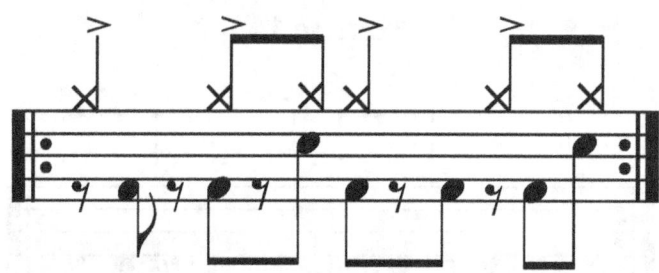

Exercise 19

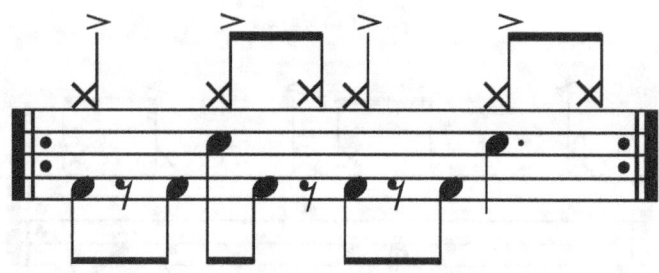

Exercise 20

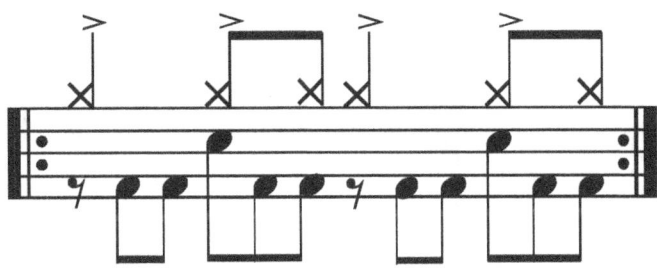

Exercise 21

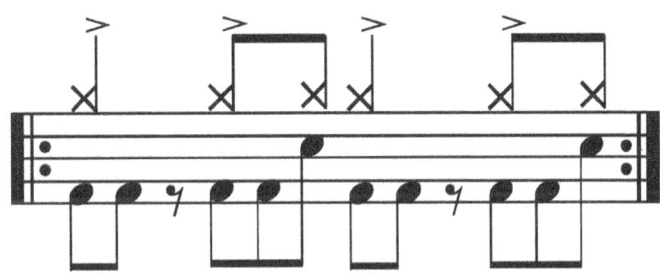

Exercise 22

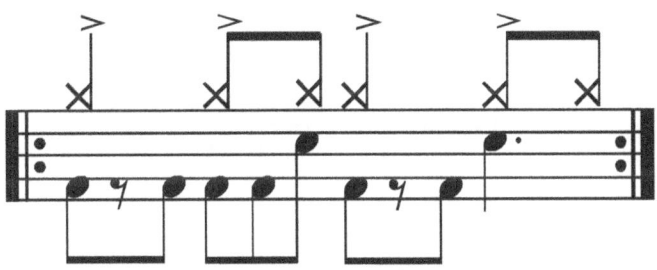

Exercise 23

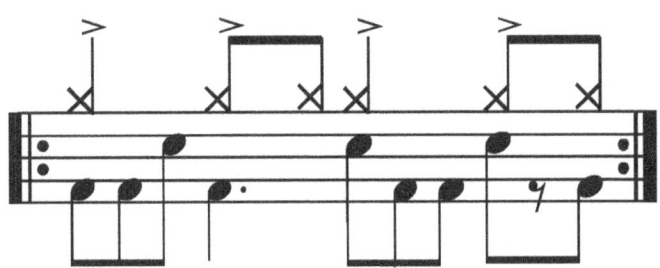

Exercise 24

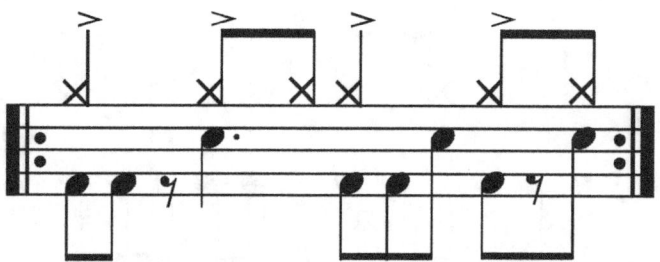

Lesson 6

Snare Drum Development Exercises

Using the Swing Beat

Remember, you should constantly thing triplets to play these exercises with accuracy. Start slowly to get a firm hold of the expected rhythms.

Exercise 1

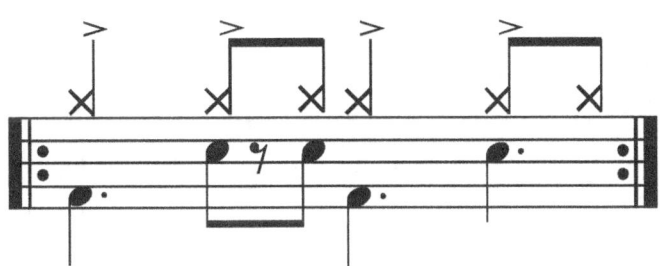

Exercise 2

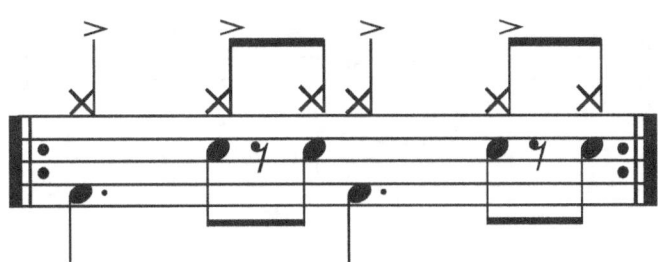

Exercise 3

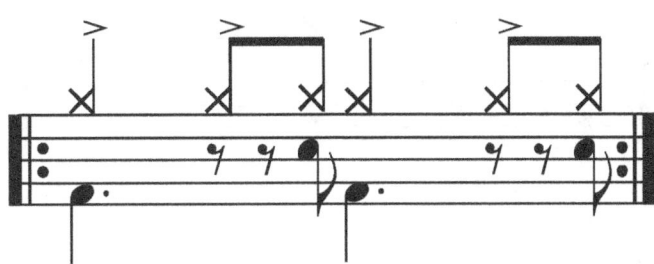

Exercise 4

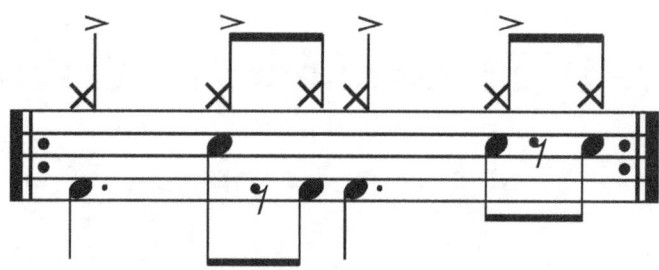

Exercise 5

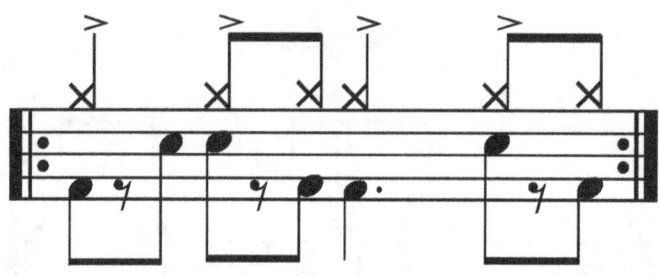

Exercise 6

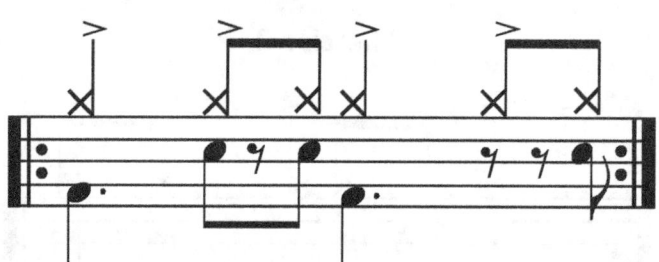

Exercise 7

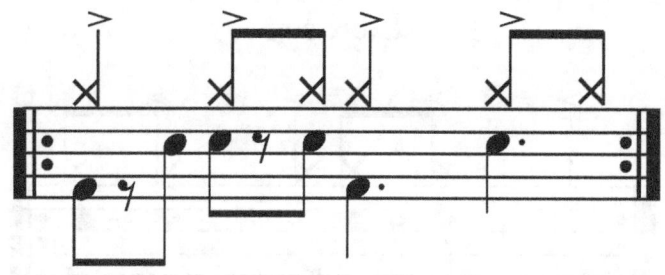

Exercise 8

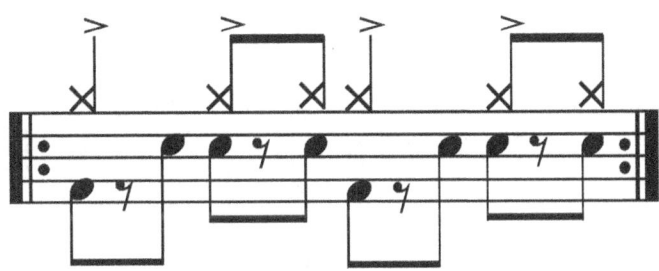

Exercise 9

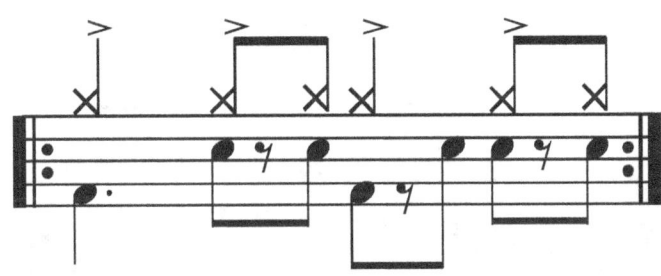

Exercise 10

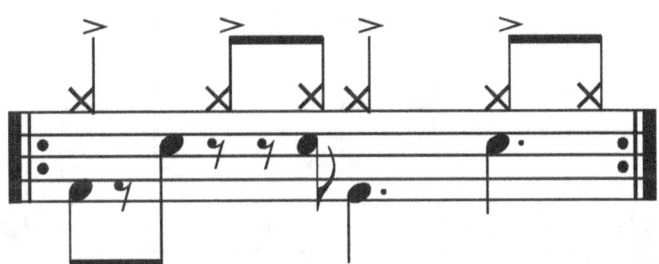

Exercise 11

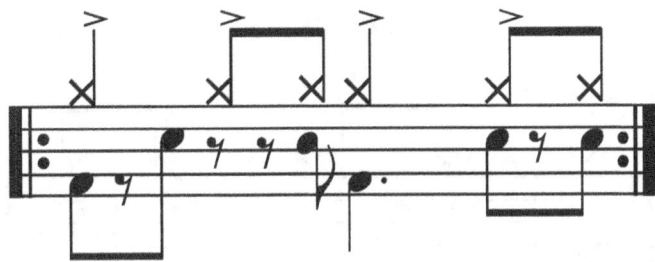

Exercise 12

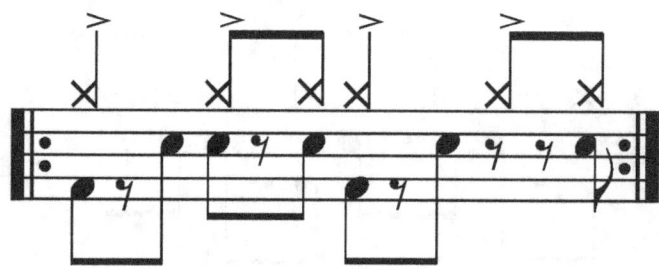

Playing the snare drum on the middle triplet.

Exercise 13

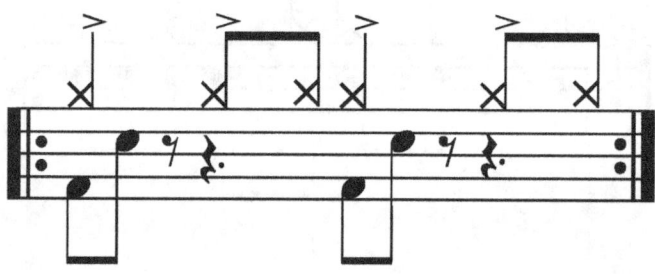

Exercise 14

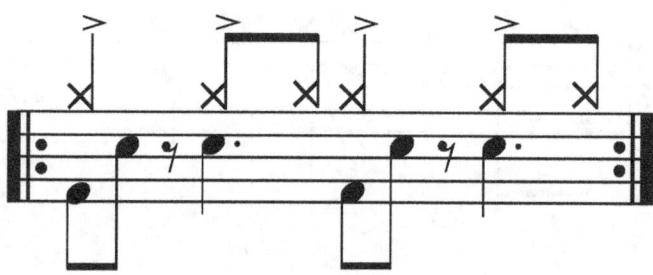

Exercise 15

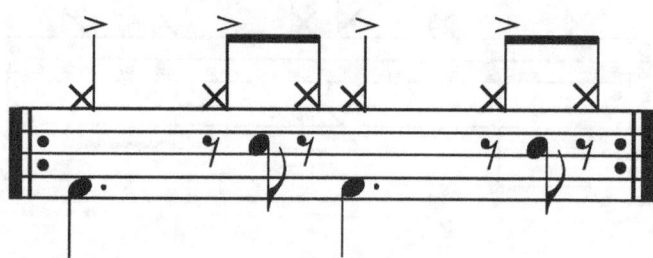

Exercise 16

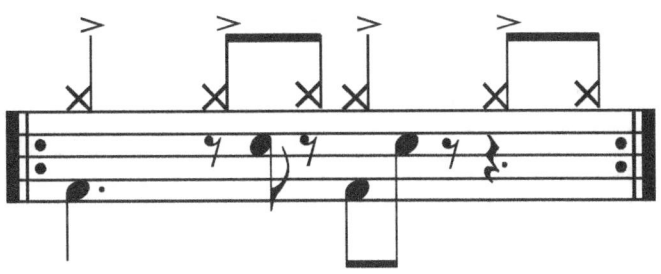

Exercise 17

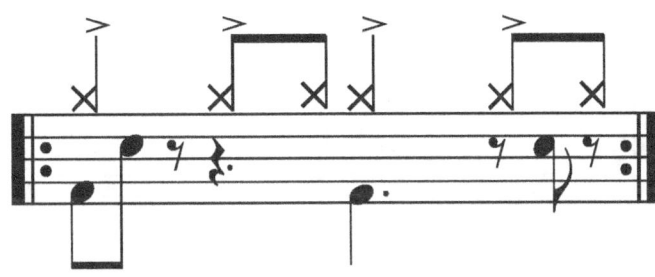

Exercise 18

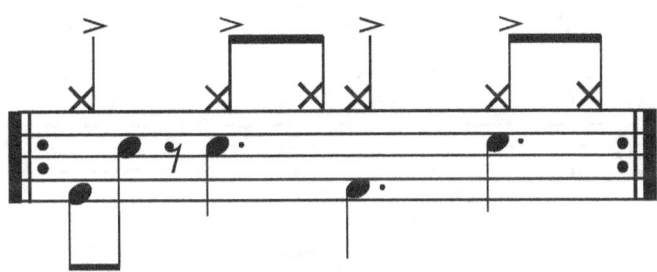

Exercise 19

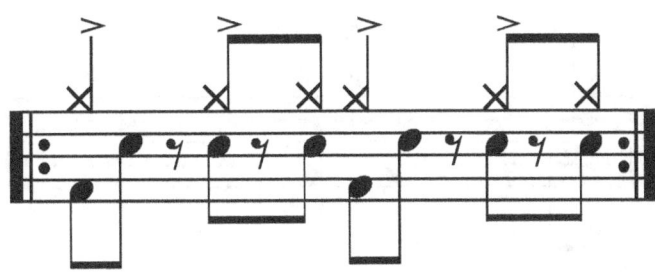

Exercise 20

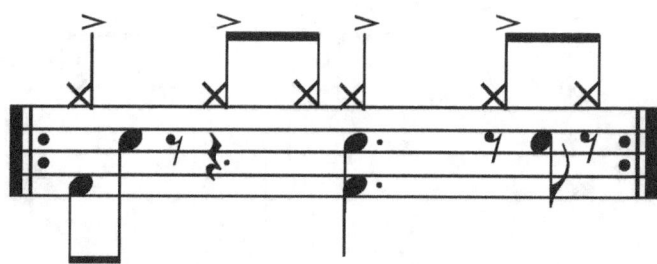

Exercise 21

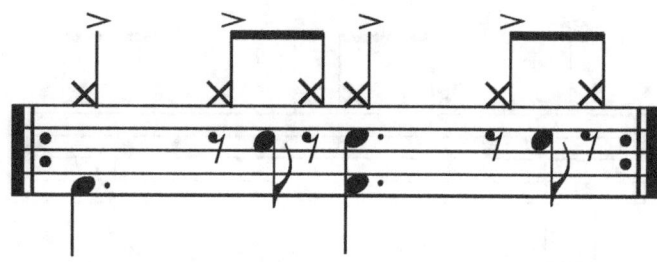

Exercise 22

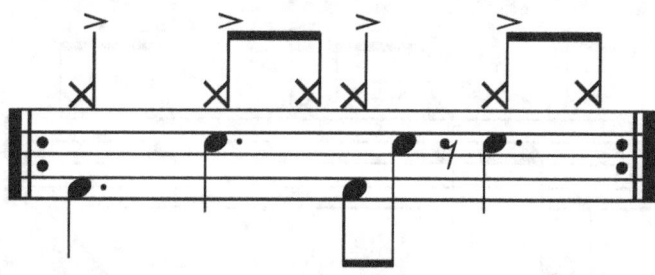

Exercise 23

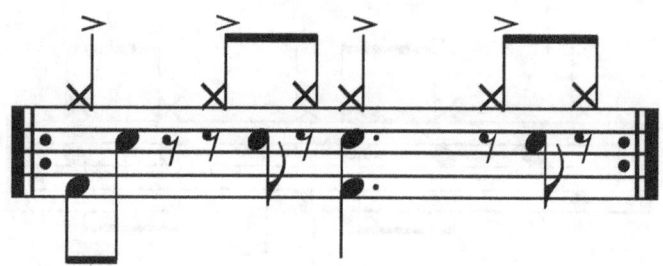

Exercise 24

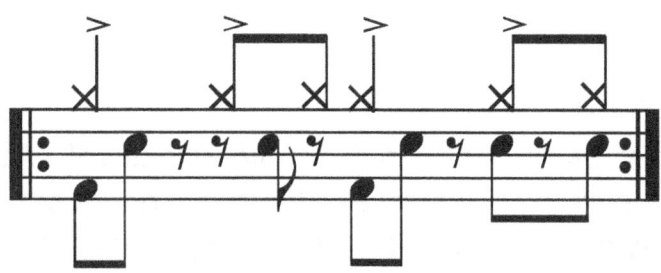

RUDIMENTARY

Flam

The flam rudiment is very similar to the double stroke roll. Actually, the produced sound is the opposite of a double stroke. Whereas the double stroke is a loud note followed by a much quieter note played with a single hand either left or right, then followed by alternate hands playing double strokes, the flam is a quiet note or grace note followed by a louder note or a note played at normal volume.

For instance, a double stroke is played like this:

R R, followed by L L, and then repeated.

However, the flam is played like this:

L R r L,

Therefore, the flow is still Right Left, Right Left but each of those is preceded by a much quieter note. Instead of just R, you play L R.

The much quieter L comes slightly before the much louder R.

This is relatively simple to play but much more complicated to explain, so don't think this is complicated at all. It is simply playing a quiet note with the left-hand followed by a normal note with the right-hand and then playing the quiet note with the right-hand followed by a normal note with the left-hand. Like we mentioned previously:

L R, r L.

You may want to practice these by playing the 1/4 note like this: R, L, R, L. But instead, you should actually play L R, r L, L R, r L.

Disciplined Practice Approach

To help you get the flams to a smooth flow, you might want to practice each flam individually. That is L R, L R, L R, L R etc.

The next step is to try with the left-hand flam like this: R L, R L, R L, R L etc.

Then when you have gotten comfortable playing each flam, left and right, you can put them together as previously explained. Finally, for your information, the flam looks like this as a written note:

A lot of the time in drumming, because of the involvement and integration of both hands or both legs and combinations between the two, you will notice a rocking or swaying motion between the limbs. For instance, when you play a left-hand flam followed by a right-hand flam and repeat this, you notice that there is a swaying from one to the other.

The swaying motion was suggested in the Modern Drumming Concepts book but I will extend that knowledge by touching on it here. The fact is that the swaying motion is the space referred to in the previously mentioned book.

This is where we begin to really notice and play the space for the first time in a practical sense and by space, I mean the movements you make to play what you play. In this case, the movement is the sway or what goes on between each flam, left then right then left then right again and so on.

Don't get too bogged down in this as it will develop naturally as you build on the rudiments and the exercises throughout the series. But just be aware of the balance points within drumming or the physics of drumming.

These balance points are suggested with the feet and leg positions, the seating positions and the way that you hold the sticks, right down to the balance of your whole core and the flow or motion you make as you sit and play the drums themselves.

Finally, understand that just like:

- Part 1 of this series was centered around the single stroke roll
- Part 2 was centered around the triplet rudiment.
- Part 3 was centered around the double stroke roll.

And this fourth book in the series is centered around integrating the rudiments covered so far.

Featured Drummer Recommendations

Steve Smith

I believe every serious drummer should be introduced to Steve Smith who was the drummer for the band called Journey for many years.

However, I have never really listened to Journey very much but I was introduced to Steve Smith when he was working for the band's Steps Ahead and Vital Information.

Please note that any recommendations I make regarding bands and drummers mostly relate to contemporary rock, fusion or jazz style music as I found it to be much more educational than pop or rock style commercial music.

Anything by the two bands I just mentioned and Steve Smith is going to be an educational experience regarding the drumming. He is simply too well coordinated to not include here or in your own studies on drummers.

Later in the Time Space and Drums series, I include some odd groupings which were most definitely Steve Smith inspired.

A good place to start learning from Steve Smith is by getting hold of his two tuition lesson videos called Steve Smith Part 1 and Steve Smith Part 2. Those DVD/videos include full songs from the bands he was working with at the time: Steps Ahead and Vital Information.

I must warn you though, if you are new to drumming or have been playing less than a year or two, I would suggest not getting bogged down by complex more advanced lessons such as those included in Steve's DVD's. Instead, you should focus on building a solid foundation so that when you do approach those advanced lessons full on, you will be more easily able to assimilate what Steve plays. In a lot of cases, this means reading the drum examples included in those DVDs.

So Why Do I Recommend Steve Smith?

Well, I included him here so as to give the student of drums a point to aim for regarding your basic rock style beats. Steve covers these in the DVDs mentioned above and demonstrates them in their most musical form, which incorporates the flowing motions you should strive to achieve with your own drumming. He demonstrates the beat styles that we are covering here in a brilliantly clear manner where drumming is not rock and it's not jazz; it's not loud and heavy but it's not too light. Everything is just smooth and flowing. And so, the aim with parts 1 to 4 of the Time Space and Drums series is really to create the very foundation that Steve Smith demonstrates on those videos. The key is Integration and flow from one to the other and back again.

However, he moves beyond those foundational beats and adds some crazy coordination exercises that should only be challenged if you have already built a solid Rock Foundation as covered here in this book series. The Time Space and Drums series really is a foundation for more advanced lessons such as those Steve includes in those DVDs. So, until you have completed this series, I suggest just taking a look at Steve Smith DVDs and checking them out. Pay special attention to the flow of the basic beats that he covers and that we have covered here. You can then develop your own style after processing his basic flow technique.

You could say that the Time Space and Drums series is the whole drumming foundation and Steve Smith's basic lessons are then the building blocks used to build and develop your own style upon that foundation. Then add Dave Weckl's Back to Basics techniques and you have the making of a pretty great drummer.

Conclusion

The importance of these beginning exercises cannot be stressed enough. You should perfect them all. This goes for every single exercise within the series. Remember, this is the beginning, so everything in the following years will depend on the degree of mastery you achieve here and now with these exercises.

As well as playing them as written and demonstrated, you should play them all again, writing them out, if necessary, with the right-hand on the ride cymbal and the left foot playing the HH.

As we did in books 1 and 2, we played everything then repeated it with the right-hand on the HH. As you progress, you will discover that the relative word will be BALANCE. Balance between the hands and feet and the RF and LF. This will place your buttocks as the pivot on which everything else is balanced. This is why the seating posture is vitally important.

You should make it a daily conscious thought when beginning to practice adjusting yourself into a playing position and hold that position when you are comfortable.

As demonstrated in the title of the first two books, GRAVITY—getting a good solid grounding—here and now is vital, but remember, this will all take time.

That being said, you should always enjoy what you are doing. But for now, you have a lot to do. You can even try writing your own rhythms as well. Be creative and experiment.

Anyway, I won't keep you any longer. Good Luck as always.

Stephen Hawkins

Closing Note:
The Time Space and Drums series is intended as a complete program from Part 1 to Part 12. It is strongly advised that you follow the program in order of the parts as they integrate and build on each other. The only thing I can now add is to practice each exercise until you have them all mastered. Mastery comes from paying attention to the most basic fundamentals already covered in each of the exercises within this book.

Once you have perfected each exercise you may like to try them left-handed but that may take time depending on your current skill level.

Free Audio Demonstrations
Please don't forget to visit the following URL to download audio demonstrations of every exercise in this book as soon as possible. You will then receive soma additional tips and guidance through the included essence emails.

www.timespaceanddrums.com/tsd-4de.html

What's Next
Thank you for choosing Time Space and Drums as one of your learning tools. I hope you enjoyed the process. You can explore more of the series in Time Warps, the fifth book in the series by searching for "Odd Time Drumming Foundation" at your favorite bookstore.

Share Your Experience

If you have a moment, please review this Jazz Drumming Development book at the store where you bought it. Help other drummers and tell them why you enjoyed the book or what could be improved. Thank you!

Thank you again dear reader and I hope we meet again between the pages of another book. Remember, You rock!

Other Books by The Author

Modern Drumming Concepts
Rock Drumming Foundation Series part. (Six in-depth Drum Lessons).
Jazz Drumming Foundation Series part. (Six in-depth Drum Lessons).
Rock Drumming Development Series part. (Six in-depth Drum Lessons).
Jazz Drumming Development Series part. (Six in-depth Drum Lessons).
Odd Time Drumming Foundation Series part. (Six in-depth Drum Lessons).
Accents and Phrasing Series part. (Four in-depth Drum Lessons).
Basic Latin Drumming Foundation Series part. (Four in-depth Drum Lessons).

 Have you ever thought about what it would feel like to make a living as a pro drummer?

If so, then visit the Drum Coach website. I might be for YOU!

The purpose of the Drum Coach blog is not only to provide drummers with valuable information but also to help them share their passions.

The Drum Coach provides all types of drumming information from beginner lessons right up to professional level playing skills, as well as personal self*(drummer)*-improvement essentials – there's something here no matter your skill level!

Some of the most important information on this website comes from my personal experiences as a percussionist and musician for over 35 years. So, I invite you to take advantage of the Drum Coach Experience, whose aim is to provide high-quality, on-demand information for drummers as they travel along their journey to achieve their personal drumming goals and ambitions.

Our commitment to our readers is always 100%! If you have any problems, questions, or concerns, just let us know and we'll help you take care of the situation as quickly as possible.

And remember to **Stay In Time!** and continue to **Rock!**